CREATION
BOOK PUBLISHERS

Third edition: 2015

For information on creation/evolution issues and materials for all ages, visit: creation.com

ISBN: 978-1-921643-52-1

One BIG family

The truth about where we all came from.

About the Authors:

Gary Bates is the CEO of *Creation Ministries International-US* (CMI) and CMI-Worldwide (CMI's international federation of ministries). Both he and his wife Frances have been involved in the creation/evolution debate for over 20 years. In his desire to deal with the influences of popular culture on our young people, Gary penned *Alien Intrusion: UFOs and the Evolution Connection*, which is still one of the most popular creation books ever written. Frances is an experienced Events Manager with CMI and has assisted Gary during his extensive speaking ministry around the world. They have been married for over 30 years and together have raised 4 adult children.

CMI is a non-denominational ministry with offices in seven countries. They seek to provide evidence-scientific and otherwise-to affirm the Genesis account of Creation and the veracity of the Bible in general. For more information please visit CREATION.com.

About the Illustrator:

Caleb Salisbury is a professional illustrator with an extensive background in game development and graphic design. He grew up in Africa and now lives in Brisbane (Australia), where he enjoys creating entertaining stories featuring whimsical characters and visually rich environments for all ages.

INTRODUCTION BY GARY AND FRANCES BATES

Our experience, after having ministered in hundreds of churches, youth groups and schools worldwide, is that many parents are simply unaware that their children have lots of tricky questions about the Bible. This is because the Bible seemingly conflicts with what they are being taught via public education, or the books they read and what they see in the secular media, for example. This book attempts to answer one of those most-asked questions, which is "Where did all the different races come from?" The idea that 'races' reflect stark built-in differences between the various people groups is not consistent with the Bible. It is a concept that was accelerated by Charles Darwin's theory of evolution and his view that people of darker skin shades were somehow less evolved than supposedly 'white' people. Modern science has now shown this to be completely false, yet the evolutionary concept about 'races' is still the dominant view of how human beings arrived here on Earth.

If we do not equip our children with answers, the world will-and it will teach them answers that assume that the world and everything in it made itself, and that no Creator was necessary. Proverbs 22:6 promises: "Train a child in the way he should go, and when he is old he will not turn from it." This should be an encouragement to all parents; with a little time and effort to help our children think biblically about these issues, we can not only immunize them against the fiery darts of the enemy, but show them there are answers they can use when they grow up, to reach others. This will ultimately make a difference in the world in which they live.

The Bible's true account of history, that all people everywhere are closely related, and are made in the image of their Creator is one of the most heartwarming and affirming messages than any person can hear.

ABOUT REFERENCES/ENDNOTES

As a help to parents, you will notice references that are linked to article titles at the back of this book. This recommended extra reading contains more in-depth explanations to help you and your children understand the concepts that are being proposed. All of these articles can be found on CMI's website (CREATION.com). As you access these initial articles you will also find they recommend additional related articles of interest for varying levels of readership.

Who is part of your family?

Who are you related to?

Is your family just your daddy and mommy and your brothers and sisters?

What about the people who live next door?
Are they part of your family?

6

What about all the people you
see when you go shopping or at school?

Are they part of your family?

What about people who live in faraway lands? They might have different looking skin and seem a bit different to you.

Are they part of your family?

Although some people look a bit different, did you know that we are much more alike than we are different to each other?

Look! We all have two arms and legs, and two eyes and ears. Try to see how much alike we actually all are.

Our differences are really very small. That's because you are related to everyone else in the world. You are part of a giant worldwide family. Yippee! But how did this happen?[1]

IN THE BEGINNING

In the very beginning the Creator God made the world. He made all the animals first.

He then made the first people.
First a man, then a woman.[2]

Genesis 1:1, Genesis 1:20-27, Genesis 2:7-23

13

God was their Father.

They were called Adam and Eve because they would become the father and mother of all people-everywhere.[3] They had middle-brown-colored skin, brown hair and brown eyes.

In those days, nobody died and there was no pain.

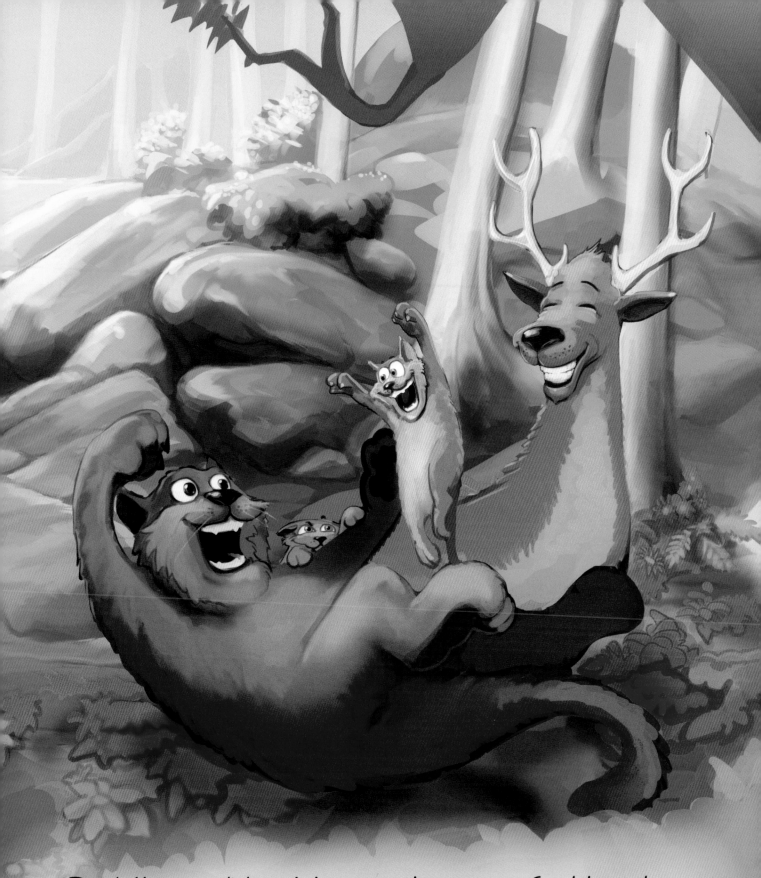

Bad things did not happen because God loved and took care of His family. Things were very good. Actually, it was all perfect!

Luke 3:38, Genesis 3:20, Genesis 1:31

But one day Adam and Eve listened to an evil angel called Satan. Satan did not love his Creator and he lied to Adam and Eve. He spoke to them through a serpent.

They believed Satan and disobeyed God. This is called sin.[4]

From that day Adam and Eve slowly began to die. Lots of bad things started to happen, because they had not listened to God.

Genesis 3:1-6, Genesis 3:16-19

They used to walk and talk with God just like you talk with your daddy and mommy. But not anymore. Adam and Eve felt really alone now— and maybe afraid, too.

God promised to send someone to save Adam and Eve's family from their sin problem. This showed that God still loved the people He had made.

Genesis 3:8, Genesis 3:22-24, Genesis 3:15

WHERE DO WE ALL COME FROM?

Adam and Eve lived for hundreds of years before they eventually died.

In that time they had lots of sons and daughters. And from their children came more and more children.

No two children were exactly the same.

Some had wide noses or narrow noses, huge ears or tiny ears. Some had black hair and some had brown. Later, some had fair hair too. Sometimes it was curly hair and sometimes it was straight.

Some grew to be very tall and some not so tall at all. And people had many different shades of brown skin and some had freckles too!

Genesis 5:4-5, Genesis 5:6-32

Some had light brown skin. They looked almost white. Others were very dark brown. They looked almost black. Some were a light yellowish brown, some more reddish brown. But most were just somewhere in between. A kind of middle brown.

Some children were born with different-shaped eyes. Many had brown eyes, just like Adam and Eve. Many generations went by, and some had blue eyes-some even had green or grey eyes.

But did you know that blue eyes are not really blue? It is because there is just less brown color in their eyes. The light makes them look blue.[5] Some time after creation, some people lost the ability to make as much brown color in their eyes.

The children looked beautiful. This was because, just like their parents, they were made in God's image.

This human family grew larger and larger. But they had a sin problem too, because they were like their parents.

The human family became selfish and mean to one another. People became so bad that God had to do something about it.

He loved the people He had made, but was saddened that their hearts became bad.

Genesis 5, Romans 5:12, Genesis 6:5-6

STARTING A NEW FAMILY... AGAIN!

Everyone was acting badly because they forgot God. God looked for one good person who still loved him.

He found Noah, who had a family of his own.

So God decided to start the world again through Noah's family. God told Noah that He would send an enormous Flood to cleanse the earth because people had made it a terrible place.[6]

27

God told Noah how to build a huge, strong ship called an Ark.[7] On the Ark, God would save Noah and his family, and all the kinds of animals too.

It took Noah and his family a long, long time to build the Ark.

When the Ark was finished the land broke up. There were earthquakes and floods and pouring rain. The Earth was destroyed. All the people and the animals outside the Ark died. It was such a shame that God had to do this.

Genesis 6:14-16, Genesis 6:18-21, Genesis 6:3, Genesis 7:11-12, Genesis 7:21-23

A NEW BEGINNING

After 150 days the water stopped rising and started to go down.

One year after the Flood began, Noah and his family got off the Ark. The animals left the Ark too, and they spread out all over the earth.

Noah's family grew with lots more children.[8] There were many, many people on the earth again.

Genesis 8:3, Genesis 8:18-19, Genesis 9:1, Genesis 10

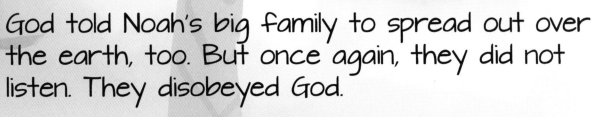

God told Noah's big family to spread out over the earth, too. But once again, they did not listen. They disobeyed God.

They wanted to live together without God and make themselves important. So they built a very tall tower to reach into the sky.[9]

But God gave many of the people different languages so they could not understand each other. This caused them to spread out all over the earth and make new families.[10]

Genesis 11:1-9

Now people could only marry others with the same language.

People with dark brown skin didn't get sunburnt. They lived best where the sun shone hotter. They married others with dark brown skin that lived close by. Some of the children got darker skin than their parents.

People with light brown skin lived best where the sunlight was not so hot. They married others with light brown skin that lived close by. Some of their children got lighter skin than their parents.

And there were people with middle brown skin who lived all over the earth. Today, everyone in our one BIG human family has different shades of brown skin. Even you![11]

All over the world, families with different languages grew and grew. They built cities and took land to make their own countries.

As time passed they learned how to do new things. They taught their children, who then learned more new things by themselves. And then their children learned more new things too.

People are very clever and can learn quickly, because God made them to be that way.

People continued to spread out and make new families and new countries.

Because they separated, their languages started to change and become even more different from each other. They made different clothes and learned to eat different foods.

They sang different songs and danced different dances. As they spread across the earth they forgot that God was the Creator. They made up different stories about where they came from. Most people forgot that they all came from one family to begin with.

2 Peter 3:5

Because all people come from one family, all people have a sin problem. They continued to do bad things just like you and me, and all people today. Although they forgot about God, He did not forget about them.

God kept His promise. He sent part of His own family to save them from their sins. He sent His one and only Son, Jesus, to be their Savior. When He came, He became part of our family. Because of that, we became part of His family too.

Because Jesus is the Son of God the Creator, He is the only One who can forgive people their sins. If you ask him, He can forgive your sin too. He will, because He promised to.

If you trust Him you will become His child. He will be your heavenly Father and you can join God's saved family. Just like when He made a way for Noah's family to be saved.[12]

Romans 3:23, John 3:16, Romans 10:9-10, John 1:12-13, Hebrews 11:7

CAN YOU SEE YOUR BIG FAMILY NOW?

All the people in the world came from one family in the beginning. Even though we are all a little different, we are all related to each other. Some people are called black. Some people are called white.

But we are really one family with many shades of brown skin. And some people have different shaped eyes. But we are mostly the same as each other.[13]

You see, your daddy and mommy had a daddy and mommy. And your grandparents had a daddy and mommy too. If we keep going back far enough, we can learn that Adam and Eve were the first daddy and mommy of all the people in the world. In many countries people still have stories about this.

And also how we all came from Noah's family who survived the great Flood.[14] The Bible has always told us how families began. And now, clever scientists can show that all people came from one family.[15] The Bible was right all along.

We are many sizes and different shapes. And we may live in faraway places. But thanks to God, our Creator, we are all part of one REALLY BIG family.

And we should thank God for that.

FOOTNOTES

[1]How could all people in the world arrive from an original pair of people? Who did their children marry? Wouldn't there be birth defects if close family members intermarried, and so on? The physical, 'racial' differences between all human beings represent a tiny fraction of our genes. Overwhelmingly, all people groups are genetically closely related, supporting the Bible's view of the history of mankind. Please read creation.com/races and creation.com/cainswife.

[2]The Bible supports the view that both men and women are equal in God's sight. But He does define specific roles for each. See creation.com/biblical-view-women.

[3]Adam and Eve were the father and mother of all the living. See children's article 'She's beautiful.' creation.com/she-is-beautiful.

[4]Satan was present at the creation of the universe and he knew that mankind was special to God. See creation.com/strategy-of-the-devil.

[5]See creation.com/interracial. Because there seems to be major differences in people groups, many have subscribed to the non-biblical view of 'race'. See creation.com/genetics-fishy.

[6]Some contend this was a local flood designed to deal with a local population problem. The language of the Bible clearly indicates this was a global event, and there is much geological evidence on the earth today to testify to this event. See creation.com/flood_waters. (Was the Flood global?)

[7]For lots of questions related to the Flood and Noah's Ark, see creation.com/noah.

[8]All humanity came from two original people, and subsequently eight people who survived the great Flood of Noah's time creation.com/grandsons. (The sixteen grandsons of Noah).

[9]The Tower of Babel event was symptomatic of mankind's desire to do and justify what is right or wrong in their own eyes. This idea is known as humanism, and it stems from the notion that there is no God or Creator to whom mankind is ultimately accountable. See creation.com/babel.

[10]Despite there being many languages on the earth today, most can be traced back to just a few distinct major language groups, once again confirming the Bible's history of the Babel group being initially separated by language by God. See creation.com/babel-linguistics.

[11]The major racial differences that most people focus on are apparent differences in skin colour. Actually we all have the same skin colour, the same brown skin pigment called melanin. But we just have different shades of brown, depending on how much of that pigment we produce. See creation.com/skin-deep.

[12]The Ark was a means of salvation to escape the coming judgment of the Flood. See creation.com/noahs-flood-why. Figuratively, the Lord Jesus Christ is another 'ark' of salvation if one believes in Him. See creation.com/good-news.

[13]People have been able to successfully receive donated organs from others belonging to people groups that appear to be very different from their own. This refutes the evolution-inspired idea that there are huge biological differences between such groups. See creation.com/blood-brothers. Also, in the right circumstances, children with the same parents, sometimes even (non-identical) twins, can appear to be from widely differing 'races'. See creation.com/two-tone-twins.

[14]Most tribal groups around the world have stories of a major, earth-destroying flood that was survived by only a few people and some animals. Many of these stories are corrupted from the biblical account. (Many tribal groups did not have writing, so the stories were passed down orally through succeeding generations.) See creation.com/many-flood-legends.

[15]Besides revealing incredible, multilayered levels of complexity, studies of human DNA reveal that all people are very closely related. See creation.com/noah-and-genetics.

This book was based upon an original idea by Ruthanne Dolezal.
Thanks to Dr Carl Wieland for his advice and editing work on this book, and to Lita
Cosner for researching some of the biblical texts and articles, and for proofreading.

Adam and Family is the true account of the world's very first family, that of Adam and Eve. It gives biblical answers to many of the questions that children have, arising from the evolutionary stories they see on TV such as:

- Where did human beings come from?
- Have we evolved from ape-men?
- What is sin and why is it wrong?
- Why is it easier to do bad things than to do good things?
- Why is there so much suffering in the world?
- Who is Satan and why does he have so much power?
- Who did Cain marry?

It also tells how we can resist temptation and live lives that are pleasing to God through having faith in Christ's death on the Cross and His Resurrection.

The Oxpecker and the Giraffe

I Need You and You Need Me

A delightful nature story in 'Dr Seuss-style' rhyme about an oxpecker bird who removes ticks and other nasties from the skin of a giraffe, for the benefit of both. With captivating artwork, it uses these two zany characters to teach about God's design, and about relationships, in a way that young children can easily understand and enjoy.

Resources available at
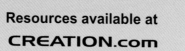